SPREAD KINDNESS with Crafts

by Ruthie Van Oosbree

a Capstone company — publishers for children

Raintree is an imprint of Capstone Global Library Limited, a company incorporated in England and Wales having its registered office at 264 Banbury Road, Oxford, OX2 7DY – Registered company number: 6695582

www.raintree.co.uk
myorders@raintree.co.uk

Text © Capstone Global Library Limited 2025
The moral rights of the proprietor have been asserted.

All rights reserved. No part of this publication may be reproduced in any form or by any means (including photocopying or storing it in any medium by electronic means and whether or not transiently or incidentally to some other use of this publication) without the written permission of the copyright owner, except in accordance with the provisions of the Copyright, Designs and Patents Act 1988 or under the terms of a licence issued by the Copyright Licensing Agency, 5th Floor, Shackleton House, 4 Battle Bridge Lane, London, SE1 2HX (www.cla.co.uk). Applications for the copyright owner's written permission should be addressed to the publisher.

Edited by Jessica Rusick
Designed by Sarah DeYoung and Denise Hamernik
Media Research by Rebekah Hubstenberger
Projects by Ruthie Van Oosbree and Chelsey Luciow
Originated by Capstone Global Library Ltd

ISBN 978 1 3982 5564 7

British Library Cataloguing in Publication Data
A full catalogue record for this book is available from the British Library.

Acknowledgements
We would like to thank the following for permission to reproduce photographs: Adobe Stock: deagreez, 4; Mighty Media, Inc.: project photos. Design elements: iStockphoto: Bakai, Dmytro Synelnychenko, mightyisland; Mighty Media, Inc.

Every effort has been made to contact copyright holders of material reproduced in this book. Any omissions will be rectified in subsequent printings if notice is given to the publisher.

All the internet addresses (URLs) given in this book were valid at the time of going to press. However, due to the dynamic nature of the internet, some addresses may have changed, or sites may have changed or ceased to exist since publication. While the author and publisher regret any inconvenience this may cause readers, no responsibility for any such changes can be accepted by either the author or the publisher.

Contents

Crafting for kindness. 4
Grow gratitude 6
The gift of words. 8
Take care package 10
Collage cards 12
Friendly fidgets 14
Affectionate affirmations 16
Creature care 18
Painting for peace 20
Wheel of kindness. 24
Woodland worry dolls 28
   Find out more 32
   About the author 32

Crafting for kindness

Do you want to change the world? Start with kindness! Whether you're hoping to show a loved one you care, raise someone's spirits or help a person or pet in need, the crafts in this book are bound to make others feel loved and appreciated. Plus, these projects are great fun to make and share. You'll love spreading kindness in your community!

What is craftivism?

Craftivism is the act of using crafts to make a change in your community. It is short for "craft activism". People make crafts to protest against issues, draw attention to causes and help build a better world. Craftivism can be used for social justice, environmentalism, peace, political change and more. Use the projects in this book to become a craftivist for a kinder world!

BASIC SUPPLIES

beads * coloured card *
decorative paper *
glue stick * hole punch *
hot glue gun *
magazines * felt-tip pens *
paint * pen and pencil *
ruler * scissors

Craftivism tips

1. **Prepare.** Collect all your materials and supplies and read through the instructions carefully before starting a project. Cover your workspace with newspaper or another covering to protect it from spills.

2. **Ask first.** Before you start crafting, get permission to use any supplies you find.

3. **Stay safe.** Ask an adult for help using hot or sharp tools or hammers. Place scrap wood under items before hammering holes into them to protect surfaces.

4. **Clean up.** Tidy up after you've finished crafting. Put supplies back where you found them, and clean up your workspace.

5. **Keep it temporary.** Craftivism projects shouldn't permanently alter public spaces. Respect these spaces and be considerate of other people!

Grow gratitude

Gratitude trees are a great way to remember everything you appreciate in life. Be kind to yourself and others by inspiring people to consider everything they're grateful for – including each other!

Supplies
- glass jar
- sand, pebbles or glass stones
- tree branches and twigs
- spray paint
- leaf-coloured card
- pencil
- scissors
- metallic marker pen
- decorative artificial branches (optional)
- pom-poms
- hot glue gun
- decorative tape

1. Fill the jar with sand, pebbles or glass stones to help the branches stand upright.

2. Spray paint the branches and let them dry.

3. Use the pencil to draw about 15 leaf shapes on the card. Cut out the leaves.

4. With a metallic marker pen, write things you are grateful for on some of the leaves. Decorate the leaves with dots, stripes, hearts and other designs if you like.

5. Place the spray-painted branches in the jar. You could add decorative artificial branches to the jar as well. Use the hot glue gun to glue pom-poms onto the branches.

6. Tape the leaves onto the branches with decorative tape.

7. Stack the remaining leaves next to the tree. Invite others to decorate the leaves by writing what they are grateful for. Then add the leaves to the gratitude tree!

CRAFTIVISM TIP

Share pictures of your gratitude tree as it grows to inspire others to take time for gratitude.

The gift of words

A short and sweet message will brighten anyone's day. And it might mean the world to someone who's feeling down! Write personalized messages for friends and family to unwrap.

Supplies

- 22 × 28-centimetre coloured card
- scissors
- ruler
- pencil with eraser
- wrapping paper
- glue stick
- ballpoint pen or felt-tip pen
- craft foam
- hot glue gun

1. Cut the card in half vertically.

2. Draw a horizontal line 7.5 cm from the top of one card. Draw a second line 18 cm from the top to divide the card into three sections.

3. Fold the card inwards along each line and unfold. Cut the top section into a rounded point like an envelope.

4. Cut a piece of wrapping paper slightly larger than the card. Use the glue stick to glue the back of the card to the wrapping paper's plain side. Let the glue dry. Trim off any extra wrapping paper.

5. Write a kind message inside the card in pencil. When you're happy with the message, trace over it in ballpoint pen or felt-tip pen. Then erase the pencil marks. Close the card by folding the bottom section up and the top section down.

6. Cut a strip of craft foam about 30 cm long and 2.5 cm wide. Draw a decorative shape, such as a bow or star, on craft foam and cut it out.

7. Wrap the strip of foam around the envelope and hot glue the ends together where they overlap. Then hot glue the decorative shape on top. You could write who the note is for on the decorative shape.

8. Repeat steps 1–7 to create more kind notes!

9

Take care package

Many people struggling with homelessness have trouble getting basic necessities. Pack up food and personal hygiene basics in a practical bag. Then donate it to a shelter!

Supplies
- duct tape in assorted colours
- medium sized freezer bag
- scissors
- hole punch
- rope or string
- care package items, such as non-perishable food, personal hygiene items and socks
- large ziplock bags
- coloured card
- felt-tip pens

1. Layer duct tape onto the ziplock freezer bag in vertical stripes of different colours. Wrap tape around the side and bottom edges to reinforce the seams of the bag. Leave the bag's seal uncovered.

2. Add a horizontal strip of duct tape along the bottom of the seal on both sides of the bag. A few centimetres of tape should hang off the edges of the bag. Stick the hanging portions of tape together to create two tabs on the sides of the bag.

3. Punch a hole in each tab. String the rope through each hole and securely knot each end.

4. Divide the care package items into separate medium-sized freezer bags – one for food and one for personal hygiene items. Place the items into the large bag.

5. Use felt-tip pens to write a kind and encouraging note on the card. Place the note in the bag.

6. Donate the care package to a local shelter or homeless organization.

CRAFTIVISM TIP

Products like a toothbrush and toothpaste, tissues, lip balm, nail clippers, menstrual products and water bottles are also great to include in a care package.

Collage cards

Many people living in care homes deal with boredom and loneliness. Create fun, kind cards to send to elderly people in your community.

Supplies

- old magazines
- scissors
- pencil with eraser
- scratch paper
- coloured card
- glue stick
- white card
- coloured pencils
- black felt-tip pen or ballpoint pen
- decorative paper

1. Cut out cute, pretty or inspiring images from the magazines. Use the pencil and scratch paper to brainstorm puns or other fun, encouraging phrases to go with the images you find.

2. Fold a piece of coloured card in half to make a card. Glue a magazine cutout inside the card.

3. Use pencil to write a message on white card. Use the ballpoint pen or felt-tip pen to trace over the words.

4. Erase the pencil lines and cut around the message. Glue the message over part of the magazine cut-out.

5. Colour in the background of the message so it blends in with the magazine cut-out. Glue accents of decorative paper or additional magazine cut-outs inside the card if you like.

6. Glue strips of decorative paper or more magazine cut-outs to the front of the card. You could add another message to the front.

7. Send your cards to a care home to brighten the days of people who could do with a little kindness!

CRAFTIVISM TIP

Some organizations collect letters to send to people in care homes. You can also contact care homes in your area to see if they will accept your cards for residents.

13

Friendly fidgets

Fidgets help reduce anxiety, lower stress and improve focus. Create your own stress balls to give to friends who need a little extra kindness or who just love to fidget!

Supplies

- empty plastic water bottle
- scissors
- balloons
- jar with wide opening
- 1 tablespoon water
- measuring spoon
- cornflour
- spoon
- card
- felt-tip pen
- hole punch
- ribbon

1. Cut the top off a water bottle to create a funnel with a wide opening. Stretch a balloon around the mouth of the water bottle.

2. Put the balloon and funnel in the jar. Add the water to the balloon.

3. Spoon cornflour into the funnel. Fill the balloon as full as you can. Periodically lift the funnel out of the jar and massage the balloon to make room for more cornflour. Then place the funnel back in the jar and continue adding cornflour.

4. Once the balloon is full, remove it from the funnel and tie it closed.

5. Write a note such as "Squeeze me" or "Squish me" on card and cut it out. Punch a hole in the card above the message.

6. Tie ribbon through the hole in the note. Then tie the note to the balloon with a double knot.

7. Repeat steps 1–6 to create more stress ball fidgets. Give them to friends so they can show themselves a little kindness and de-stress!

Keep crafting!

You can craft all kinds of fidgets to help ease friends' anxieties. Make a bracelet out of a zip. Put beads on string or pipe cleaners and knot each end. Or look up instructions for making your own fidget spinner!

Affectionate affirmations

Many people struggle with negative thinking and self-doubt. Give them a constant reminder of their best qualities with a colourful keychain they can take wherever they go.

Supplies
- scratch paper
- pencil
- letter beads
- pony beads
- decorative charm
- keychain ring
- thin wire
- wire cutters
- ruler
- needle-nose pliers

1. Brainstorm positive affirmations using pencil and scratch paper. Think about who the keychain is for and what that person should remember every day.

2. Arrange the letter beads to spell out the affirmation. Add pony beads in between words and a charm to the end.

3. Cut a piece of wire about 40 cm long. Fold the wire in half. Bend the looped end around the keychain ring. Thread the ends of the wire through the loop and pull tightly.

4. String one pony bead onto both pieces of wire. Then add the affirmation you arranged in step 2.

5. String the loose ends of wire through the loop on the charm and wind them tightly.

6. Trim off extra wire and use pliers to turn any sharp edges down. Give the keychain to a friend to remind them that they're loved!

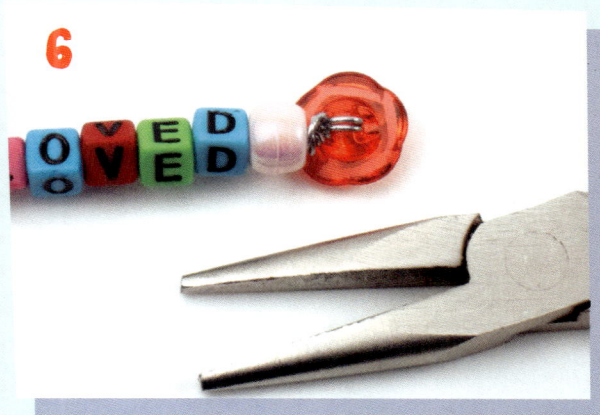

Creature care

Humans aren't the only ones who need kindness. Show a shelter animal some love by donating a soft handmade bed for it to snuggle in.

Supplies
- 1 metre solid-colour fleece, washed
- 1 metre printed fleece, washed
- scissors
- sewing pins
- ruler
- washable marker pen
- machine-washable polyester fibre fill

1. Cut both pieces of fleece to 90 × 110 cm. They can be longer or shorter in either direction as desired, as long as the measurements are even numbers.

2. Lay the solid-colour fleece face down. Lay the printed fleece face up on top of it. Line up the corners. Pin every 5 cm or so along each side to keep the layers in place.

3. With the ruler and marker pen, mark every 5 cm along each side, starting from the corners.

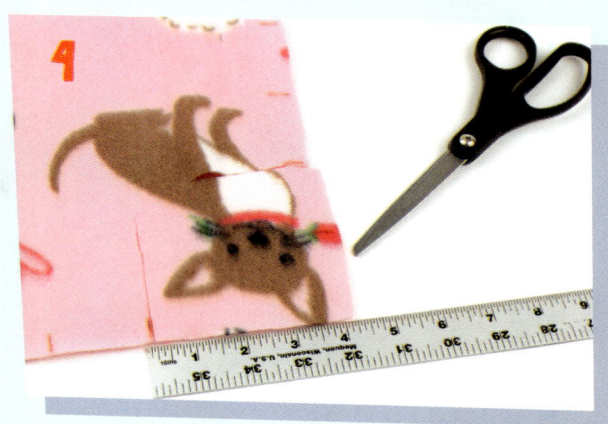

4. Using the marks as a guide, cut 10-cm squares out of each corner.

5. At each remaining mark, cut inwards from the edge about 10 cm to create fleece tassels. Remove the pins as you go.

6. Knot the top and bottom tassels together on three sides. Leave one side untied for stuffing.

7. Stuff the bed with the polyester fibre fill. The bed should provide support without being overly stuffed and puffy.

8. Knot the remaining tassels. Donate the bed to a local animal shelter to help a pet in need!

CRAFTIVISM TIP

Contact your local animal shelter to see what items they need. This knot-tying method can also be used to make blankets for homeless shelters or children's hospitals.

Painting for peace

Paint a colourful sign to make your kind or hopeful message stand out.

Supplies

- stretched canvas
- spray bottle with water
- acrylic paint in assorted colours and paintbrushes
- cotton buds
- yarn needle
- white or brightly coloured yarn

1. Spray water lightly onto the canvas. Paint a wide yellow streak diagonally across the centre of the canvas.

2. Spray the canvas with water again and paint orange on both sides of the yellow streak. The colours should touch and mix.

3. Continue adding colour streaks, spraying the canvas with water between each colour. Add red next, then purple, blue and green.

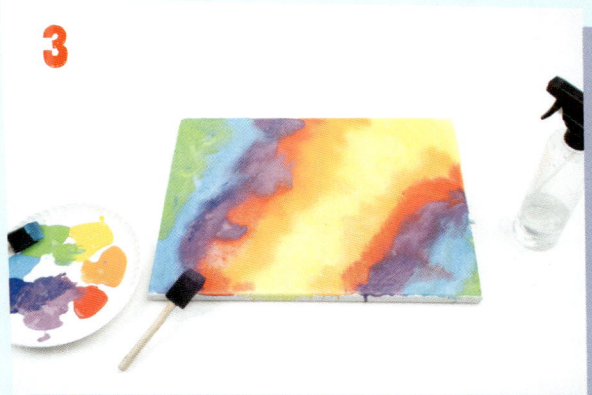

Project continues on the next page.

4. Use a small paintbrush to touch up any blank spots. Spray the canvas with water and tip it to one side so the paint colours run into each other.

5. Use the cotton buds to dab paint circles onto the matching colour sections. The circles will add depth and detail to the painting. Let the canvas dry.

6. Paint a kind word or phrase across the canvas in black letters. Let the paint dry.

CRAFTIVISM TIP

Make your peaceful painting on poster paper and cover it with clear packing tape to weatherproof it. Put it in your garden or bring it to a rally!

7. With the yarn needle, poke a hole about every 1.2 cm around one letter, making sure to get in the corners. Thread the needle with yarn. Push the needle up through one hole and down through another. Continue this process to stitch around the letter. When you've finished outlining the letter, knot the yarn on the back of the canvas. Cut off any extra yarn. Repeat this process to outline the remaining letters.

8. If you like, paint the sides of the canvas black for a polished look.

9. Hang your peaceful painting up to show love and kindness to anyone who sees it. Or give it as a gift!

Keep crafting!

Add more yarn to your painting! Stitch extra yarn accents onto your painting, such as stripes that match the background. You could even use yarn instead of paint to spell out your message.

Wheel of kindness

Performing a random act of kindness means helping and being nice to others without expecting anything in return. Randomise your acts of kindness with this spinner!

Supplies

- large circular plastic lid or plate
- jar lid
- hammer and nail
- paint and paintbrush
- bolt
- 2 washers
- nut
- scissors
- coloured paper
- PVA glue
- hot glue gun
- cardboard
- magnet
- pencil
- circular item for tracing
- pen
- clear tape
- gems

1. Use the hammer and nail to make holes in the centres of the two lids.

2. Paint the jar lid in a solid colour. Let the lid dry.

3. Slide a washer onto the bolt. Push the bolt through the top of the larger lid.

CRAFTIVISM TIP

Make two wheels: one to put on the fridge at home and another to put in your locker at school, if you have one. Write different acts of kindness for the different places where you'll hang the wheels.

Project continues on the next page.

4. Slide another washer onto the bolt. Screw the bolt through the top of the jar lid.

5. Place a nut on the end of the bolt. Check that the large lid can spin while you hold the jar lid still. If it cannot, loosen the nut or use a longer bolt.

6. Take the wheel apart. Cut an arrow out of coloured paper and glue it to the painted side of the lid. The arrow's point should go over the edge of the lid. Reassemble the wheel.

7. Using the hot glue gun, glue small pieces of cardboard to the back of the wheel to create a surface for the magnet. Make sure the cardboard is level with the jar lid's edges so the magnet will be able to touch surfaces. Hot glue the magnet to the cardboard.

8. Trace circles onto different colours of paper. Make sure they fit between the jar lid and the edge of the larger lid. Cut the circles out.

9. Add gems to decorate the wheel. Write an act of kindness on each circle in pen. Then tape the circles to the lid.

10. Hang the wheel on a magnetic surface. Spin it whenever you'd like to do something kind!

Keep crafting!

Once you've done all the acts of kindness on your wheel, make new circles with new acts of kindness to replace the old circles on the wheel.

Woodland worry dolls

Worry dolls come from a Guatemalan tradition. According to legend, you can tell a worry doll what's troubling you and put it under your pillow. Give one to a friend to help ease their worries.

Supplies
- small and medium wooden beads
- paint (fur colours) and paintbrushes
- pipe cleaners (fur colours)
- ruler
- paper straws
- scissors
- permanent marker pen
- craft foam (fur colours, pink)
- glue
- felt
- washable marker
- yarn or small pom-poms

1. Paint one medium wooden bead and four small wooden beads in the same colour. Let them dry.

2. Fold a pipe cleaner in half. String both ends through the medium wooden bead and pull them almost all the way through. Bend the folded end over the bead to secure.

3. Underneath the bead, fold the two ends of the pipe cleaner apart so they are horizontal. String a small wooden bead on each end about 2 cm from the medium wooden bead. Fold the pipe cleaner back towards the centre, creating arms with wooden beads for paws.

4. Cut a piece of straw about 2.5 cm long. Pull the ends of the pipe cleaner through the straw.

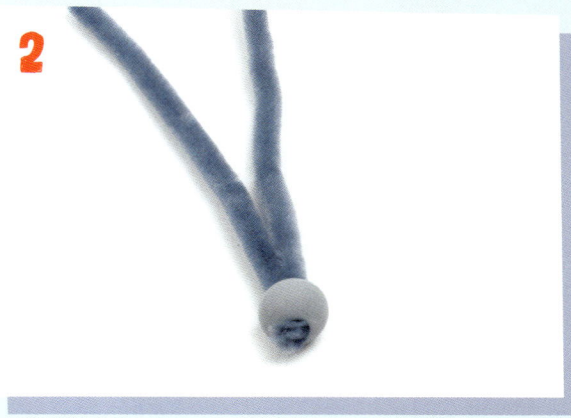

Project continues on the next page.

5. String a small wooden bead onto each end of the pipe cleaner, creating legs with wooden beads for paws. Fold about 0.5 cm of the pipe cleaners behind the beads to secure.

6. Draw a face on the head with permanent marker pen.

7. Cut out craft foam ears for the worry doll. Cut small pink pieces of craft foam to glue inside the ears. Glue both ears onto the head.

8. Fold a piece of felt in half. Lay the worry doll on the felt. Use washable marker pen to trace an outline of a piece of clothing, such as a shirt, trousers, a dress or overalls, around the doll.

9. Cut the piece of clothing out of both layers of felt. Hot glue the two pieces together around the worry doll. Repeat with additional clothing items.

10. Glue a yarn or pom-pom tail (depending on the animal) onto the felt.

11. Repeat steps 1–10 to make additional animals. Give the worry dolls to your classmates to help them put their minds at ease!

9

10

Keep crafting!

Make human worry dolls with painted beads and pipe cleaners in various skin tones. Use colourful embroidery thread to create fun hairstyles!

Find out more

Books

10-Minute Crafty Projects, Lucy Makuc and Elsie Olson (Raintree, 2021)

How to Make a Better World, Keilly Swift (DK Children, 2020)

Mini Gifts that Surprise and Delight (Mini Makers), Lauren Kukla (Raintree, 2024)

Websites

www.bbc.co.uk/cbbc/curations/bp-arts-and-crafts-collection
The CBBC website has lots of craft projects to make.

www.goodhousekeeping.com/home/craft-ideas/g20967550/summer-crafts/
Check out this website for lots of different craft ideas for you to try.

About the author

Ruthie Van Oosbree is a writer and editor who loves making crafts. She is passionate about social justice, animal welfare and the environment. She lives with her husband and three adorable cats.